GW01458293

You Can Be Thin!

SLENDERNESS THROUGH PSYCHOLOGY

By HERMAN FRIEDEL, M.D.

Foreword by
MILTON JACOVY, M.D.

——◄◄●►►——

1948

Caxton House, Inc.

NEW YORK

Printing Statement:

Due to the very old age and scarcity of this book,
many of the pages may be hard to read due to the
blurring of the original text, possible missing pages,
missing text and other issues beyond our control.

Because this is such an important and rare work, we
believe it is best to reproduce this book regardless of
its original condition.

Thank you for your understanding.

Contents

————◆◀●▶◆————

[_v_]

Foreword

———◆◄●►◆►———

DIETARY PROBLEMS and the question of obesity have long occupied an important place in our daily lives. Popular interest has been stimulated mainly by esthetic considerations. Scientific concern over obesity, however, stems from the realization by medical men that several bodily disorders—somatic diseases—such as hypertension, heart disease, and diabetes are particularly prone to occur in stout individuals, and that the course of the illness is unfavorably influenced by their extra weight.

A common misconception among many people is that endocrine (glandular) factors are chiefly responsible for obesity and that food intake is only incidental at best. This has promoted a defeatist attitude which has led many to a "laissez-faire" policy—while they tipped the scales at ever increasing weights. Though few students of the subject completely deny the importance of glandular activity in metabolism, their shift of emphasis to dietary factors has led to a greater understanding of obesity and to the valuable knowledge that a great deal can be accomplished to cure it.

During the last decade, research in psychosomatic medicine—the study of the relationship between mind and body—has thrown the entire problem of obesity into sharp relief. The statement: "People are stout because they eat more and consume more calories" no longer suffices. Now we ask: *"Why* do some individuals eat more?"

For it has been proved that abnormally large consumption of food is undeniably related to emotional problems and personality difficulties. Obesity is as revealing of a maladjustment as any neurotic symptom; as, for example, a phobia or an hysterical complaint. A proper understanding of one's emotional difficulties, plus a correct modification of diet, is essential to the solution of the problem of obesity. The attack must be on two fronts—the dietary and the psychological.

Dieting has notoriously been a difficult task. Certain emotional needs are satisfied by food, and it is not easy to give up one's satisfactions. This has tempted many to take short-cuts, to use harmful drugs, instead of to attack directly and limit food intake. Many uninformed dieters prejudice their chances for success by eating the wrong kinds of food, losing precious minerals and vitamins in their undirected slimming efforts. Education in elementary dietetics, then, becomes absolutely essential for those who wish to combat their obesity.

You Can Be Thin: Slenderness through Psychology has handled the problem of the care and cure of obesity lucidly and interestingly. The emphasis is clear and well-founded. The *how's* and the *why's* of the obesity problem receive their just due. A thoroughly practical instrument for education, this book points the way to better physical and mental health as well as to intelligent weight-reduction.

MILTON JACOVY, M.D.

CHAPTER I

*In Which You Are Led
to the Starting Point*

———— ◆◄●►◆ ————

YOU OPEN this book hopefully but doubt-
fully. You've been on diets before.
They've all failed. Or, rather, you've failed
to keep any of them.

Sometimes that really may have been
the fault of the diet itself. It may have been
the sort of one a martyr would find difficulty in keeping. And you're only an ordi-
nary human being—even if you do occasionally eat extraordinarily.

Usually, though, the fact that you went

off the prescribed regimen was due to a kind of balance of pleasures. The prospective pleasure of being beautifully bulge-less was less powerful than the present pleasure of eating what—and as much as—you wanted to. Even the ridicule of your acquaintances and the (perhaps more painful) pleasantries of your friends couldn't change the balance.

Right now is the time to tell a basic psychological truth. Until *you develop insight into the causes* for your excessive eating—you'll almost certainly fail to keep any course of dieting you embark upon. *BUT:* develop that insight, get to understand the reasons you reach for a sweet (or a sandwich), and you've taken the first, most important step toward slenderness.

Of course, you also need a reasonable diet. By "reasonable" we *don't* mean a pro-

[2]

gram that requires an adding machine and superhuman will-power. We mean a program based on psychological fact as well as food-values.

The chapters that follow have two main purposes: *first,* to help you acquire the insight you need; and, *second,* to suggest a safe, sure, scientific reducing diet.

Now let's get to the starting point.

CHAPTER II

In Which You Gain Insight in Order to Lose Weight

———◆◄●►◆———

HERE'S A FIRST principle: you're over-weight because you overeat. (Take so much for granted now; in Chapter V you'll find all the proof of the principle you require.)

The strategic question, then, is why you overeat. Here are some of the answers. Consider them carefully, because at least one of them is an answer that carries a lot of weight for you.

[*4*]

1. You are insecure.

That's the answer for most people. They feel that they're unloved, or that they're not loved as much as they want to be. From the time they suckled at their mothers' breasts, they've had a private equation: Food = Security. So, feeling insecure, they attempt to substitute one element of the equation for another. By taking in huge quantities of food, they suppose (unconsciously, of course) that they're assimilating security too.

That's why a child who feels that his mother has rejected him—that she no longer loves him—stuffs himself sick. That's why a wife who suspects that her husband's love is on the wane gorges herself ungainly. That's why a man whose sweetheart has turned him down begins to

[5]

eat an abnormal quantity of food (or to drink an abnormal quantity of whisky, for that matter). All of them are overcompensating. They're attempting to buy back their lost security with false coin.

Sometimes the reason is economic—financial insecurity of one kind or another. Her boss is nasty, intimates that she's a very dispensable employee; and the secretary goes on a sundae-splurge.

Refugee children, on first coming to this country, ate as if they wanted to make up for the years of cruel hunger which they had suffered. When they were sent to foster-homes where they were treated kindly and understandingly, after a while their appetites bore a normal relation to their body-needs. If, however, having become acclimated to this land of (relative) plenty, they went to other foster-homes where they were treated with neither kindness nor understanding, they again began to devour food ravenously. These children, though they didn't know it, were trying to eat security, have it become a part of them.

"But," you say, "I feel secure. My husband (or wife) loves me. My job's safe enough. I've always eaten a lot. Guess I'm just naturally a big eater, and doing what comes naturally."

Before you make your mind up, think over the second reason for excessive eating.

2. You are possessed by a bad habit.

Sometimes mothers like their children too much; sometimes too little. Paradoxically, both attitudes often have the same end result: the children are overfed. In the one case, the mother takes no chances that the child is not getting enough to eat—and so he gets far more than enough. In the other case, the mother wants to atone for her lack of love (which she considers wrong) by excessive zeal in feeding him.

When the child co-operates or complies —and usually he's forced to—a pattern is eventually established. The child gets the overeating habit, and it stays with him until he takes active and energetic measures to break it.

Often, however, not the force of parental persuasion but rather the force of parental example causes the child to eat more than he needs to. He admires his gormandizing father (or mother, or older brother, or uncle), and admiration leads to imitation. Moreover, it is easier to copy his father's gallant trenchering than it is to copy his other forms of gallantry.

As the child grows older, he may come to realize that not everything about an ad-

[8]

mirable person is necessarily admirable. He may wish that he had chosen to emulate something other than his father's tendencies at table. But by this time he's been possessed by the habit. He has to dispossess himself.

3. You lack a vital interest.

You must certainly have noticed how, when you've nothing you consider worth doing, your food intake goes all the way up. You eat to kill time and not because you want to eat. This cause for overweight is particularly important for idle women. They gobble candies as a nervous gesture —often quite automatically, so that they can't remember a thing about it later. When their scales tell them that they've been over-indulging, they tell their husbands that the scales are wrong. Why, they never do more than nibble at meals! Their

[9]

husbands may listen and believe; but the scales won't.

4. You are afraid.

For a great variety of reasons, people unconsciously try to disqualify themselves from the wars of daily life. They want to show sufficient cause for not competing in games or in love. So they eat for the purpose (a purpose they never admit to themselves) of getting so fat that competition becomes impossible for them.

A boy, for example, is afraid of getting hurt while playing baseball or football. He can't tell people he's afraid—he can't even tell himself. Consequently, he eats until he becomes so unwieldy that even the thought of him running to first base is ridiculous. Only if he looks hard and long at his motives, without attempting to find excuses for himself, will he come to realize why he's impelled to have another slice of cake when he's not even remotely hungry.

Or a girl may dislike men—not necessarily in a homosexual way, but maybe because she's learned to be afraid of them through some combination of events, or because she's never become completely mature emotionally. Yet everybody expects her to go out with fellows—they consider it the normal thing to do and she doesn't disagree. To become so grossly fat that no fellow will want to take her out— that solves her problem. She won't be blamed by other people and she won't blame herself. Again, it requires keen and honest probing for her to uncover her unconscious motives.

5. You are eating neither well nor wisely.

Beans, bread, rice, spaghetti, potatoes, and other starchy foods supplied the basis of the meals of many who were brought up during the depression years. Such foods were inexpensive; they filled you; they stayed with you. Also, mother made them, you were young and usually hungry, and they tasted good. Better times came, but your early taste-training remained. You still like the starchy foods best and they still seem the only foods worth the name. So you keep eating them, even though you since have learned what you can never bring yourself wholly to believe: that starches are only one element of a balanced diet and that too many starches unbalance the diet.

Perhaps no economic stresses molded your food habits. You always had enough spending money, and you spent it as you chose . . . on candy, cake, and ice cream. You've since developed your sweet tooth until it has grown stronger than your sense of logic. Knowing that sweets ought to be only an incidental item in your diet, you've nevertheless made them a staple one.

Sometimes the process of munching sweets is so casual—even if so frequent— that people who engage in it aren't aware of the fact unless it's brought specifically to their attention. One way in which it's brought to their attention is by the groans their husbands (and their floors) emit.

CHAPTER III

In Which You Have Opened for You a Subject of Immense Practical Importance: The Psychology of Weight-Reduction

INSIGHT IS the starting point. Unless you realize that excessive eating is the *effect* of some personality *defect,* you can't hope to remedy the defect and thus eliminate the effect. You must see clearly that you eat too much because there's some gap between what you want and what you have, and that by eating too much you're trying to bridge the gap.

Your efforts are of course useless, since effects can't be eliminated without eliminating their causes. Look at that last state-

[*14*]

ment a little closer. Here's an effect: your car doesn't go. Here's the cause: you've no gas in the tank. You don't attempt pushing the car; that would be eliminating the effect only. You fill the tank with gas; that's eliminating the cause.

Your efforts to bridge the gap between *I want* and *I have* by overeating are really worse than useless. Because—by overeating you actually widen the gap: You increase your insecurity; you confirm a bad habit; you go further from a vital interest; you disqualify yourself more emphatically; you step back a greater distance from an intelligent diet. Briefly, you allow all the causes mentioned in Chapter II to take deeper root.

Suppose, for example, that you lack the security you want; and suppose that, for you (as for most people), it may be found

in marriage. A disfiguring excess of fat—
the inevitable result of eating to excess—
diminishes your chance to become secure,
since it diminishes your chance to attract
a suitable member of the opposite sex. (In
our society, obesity is not considered attractive.) Of course, you are unhappy
about the situation: so you persist in eva-
sion—you eat even more.

You've drawn a circle, a vicious circle.
The only way to break it is to attack the
fundamental cause—not the habit of overeating solely, but the cause.

To uncover the cause, you've got to
probe as mercilessly as if you were a
surgeon—and the wound someone else's.
What makes you discontent? Is it that
you're asking more than you've any right
to? Do you imagine yourself a unique act
of creation—someone specially favored?

Do you feel rebuffs with abnormal acuteness because you think yourself specially favored? Are you accomplishing less than you should because you are undertaking more than you should? Have you stayed fixed to a juvenile group of attitudes, never really attaining emotional maturity? These are specimens of the questions you must ask yourself. Just asking them—let alone giving ruthlessly honest answers to yourself—hurts. But it's a necessary pain; and the rewards are great.

A tremendous number of causes can be eliminated by intelligent self-analysis and by acting as the analysis dictates. Some, unfortunately, can't be. However, a strong dash of reason makes even these bearable.

Let's look at a case-history. (Others will be found following Chapter XV.) His name: Quentin Q. He's 33 years old when we first meet him, and he's an army draftee —or inductee, if you prefer. Before he was inducted, he'd been a fairly successful small-businessman. Quentin is of normal intelligence, or slightly higher. He's married and has two children. He's a private— and he's desperately unhappy.

His sergeant and his officers are thoroughly unsympathetic, and with the men in his company he has few points of contact. He misses his home and his family and his business. Just about the only pleasure he can discover is in eating. He supplements his company-mess by the Post Exchange, where he devours hot-dogs and guzzles pop in amazing quantities (quantities amazing even to him).

In spite of the increased activity, the drill, the hikes, the fatigue-duty, he notices that he's developing a paunch.

Well, what can Quentin do? Quit the army? Hardly. Go AWOL? Many did, under similar circumstances, but Quentin knows that such an action would be both disgraceful and unavailing.

One day Quentin is rude to an officer and he's restricted to quarters. Of course, he's pretty angry at first. After a while, though, he begins to take thought. It's not often that he's rude. Why was he this time?

Gradually, his actions assume a pattern for him. He's been thinking all along that the army has no right to keep him. But why? Aren't many, very many, of his buddies in a worse fix? Why should he consider himself a special case? Is it because his former career has been easy and protected? Because he resents any change?

Quentin realizes that he has the tendency to make his answers excuse him. He

[*19*]

avoids the soothing answer, however, and continues to try for the honest one. His searching questions reveal a mass of motives he doesn't like to admit. Nevertheless, he faces up to them. And in doing so, he learns for himself what it would be very nearly impossible for anyone to teach him.

Quentin remembers the homely saying: What can't be cured must be endured. The army offers him a harder and less pleasant life, but one that isn't completely devoid of interest and, in any event, one he's got to accustom himself to. Deliberately, he attempts to join his group, become part of something larger than himself. He makes friends, slowly at first, but after a while easily. He takes a new interest in his job and becomes proficient in it. He discovers, with something of a shock, that (though he misses home as much) he dislikes the army less—in fact, he almost likes certain phases of army life.

His visits to the Post Exchange for the purpose of stuffing himself were the product of boredom, self-pity, and a vague, generalized unhappiness. Now, with new interests, new motivations, the army-mess contents him; his trips to the P.X. become less frequent.

Quentin is not a figment of the imagination. He's a real person, and the process we've described really took place. Quentin can be your guide: his method can be your method and his triumph yours.

One essential difference, though, needs a note. Quentin's overeating was of recent origin when he began his self-analysis. Yours may be of long-standing. Consequently, you'll have some habit-breaking to do also.

[21]

CHAPTER IV

◆

*In Which You Learn a Five-Point
Program of Habit-Breaking*

————◆◄◆►◆————

IN THE PRECEDING chapter, you learned
that in order to solve your problem, you
first had to face it squarely. Running away
only intensifies it. In this chapter you're
going to learn how to proceed from that
point, how to break your overeating habit.
(Though the emphasis is on the overeating
habit, the method suggested applies to almost all other habits you want to break as
well.)

Here is an effective 5-point program.

[22]

1. You must develop an engrossing interest.
Psychology tells you firmly that breaking a bad habit is best accomplished by
putting a good habit in its place. If, for example, you're a born "knocker," always
criticizing people, force yourself to say a
few words of praise about them. In breaking your overeating habit, forming a new
habit as a substitute is even more necessary. The reason is plain: your habit is in
large part the result of boredom. Develop
a new, absorbing interest and you'll not be
bored as often. Whenever you get the im-
pulse to deplete the food-supply, deliberately engage in your substitute pursuit.
What that pursuit is, doesn't really matter:
solve chess problems or crossword puzzles,
collect stamps or trolley transfers, build
trains from matchsticks or fit ships into
small-necked bottles, sew fancy stitches or

tie fancy knots, read history or housing statistics, write poetry or letters to the editor. The important thing is: get in some new groove that can hold you, and continue along it with all the momentum you can raise.

2. Commit yourself to a diet.

Tell your family and your friends that you're going on a diet. Bet anyone who dares to that you'll keep it. Put a clear statement of your intentions concerning the diet on paper and look at it daily. The reason for all those maneuvers is to bolster your purpose and to add embarrassment to all the other penalties that failure would entail.

3. Focus on the penalties of failure and the rewards of success.

In Chapter V there's a complete discussion of the penalties of obesity. Here we need but quote the summary of Drs. Wilkins and Boyd. Useless fat, they say, "overworks the heart, tires the feet, disturbs the conscience, and decreases the attractiveness of the individual." Slimness is not only esthetically more pleasing, but also a far more healthful physical and mental state, as all insurance companies will tell you.

4. Start your diet at once.

Don't try the "tapering off" method. In breaking the overeating habit, it just doesn't work. You must decide on a fixed goal and you must proceed to it in the most direct way possible. If you say on Monday that you'll eat less on Tuesday, still less on Wednesday, and so on—the probability is that on Friday you'll be eating as much as ever. The time to begin your diet is one hour from now—about the time it will take you to finish the rest of this book!

5. Allow no exceptions.

Let Professor Rush, a noted psychologist, speak: "Every time you fail you go back nearly to where you started. It is like dropping a ball of yarn that you have been winding up or upsetting a box of tacks that you have just picked off the floor. Don't let yourself fail even once. At any particular moment you are most likely to do what you did last in the same situation." That doesn't mean that you can't ever go home for Thanksgiving or attend a Rotary dinner. But it does mean that you've got to exercise moderation at such events, and atone for all excess calories you've taken in. In Chapter XIV we'll explain the matter fully.

[26]

CHAPTER V

In Which a Number of Authorities
Persuade You, First, That Glands
Do Not Cause Obesity and, Second,
That Obesity Predisposes You to a
Variety of Ills

————◄◄■►►————

YOU MAY BE holding back because you've
heard something about excess weight being due to over-active glands rather than
over-active appetites. Let some of the ex-
perts give you the straight facts.

Dr. Frank A. Evans: "Obesity can be
caused by nothing but over-eating and can
be prevented only by avoiding that."

Dr. Lewis H. Wolberg: "Ninety-seven
percent of the cases of overweight are in

no way connected with endocrine disturbances."

Dr. Nathan W. Shock: "Although much has been written about the endocrine basis of obesity, the stark physiological fact remains that the accumulation of fat takes place only when the caloric intake is in excess of the energy used."

Simply, then, you gain weight only when you take in more fuel (in the form of food) than you burn up. When you eat more food than you need for your energy-expenditures, the surplus is stored as fat. Fat is hoarded fuel.

Did someone ask what's wrong with that sort of hoarding? One answer is obvious: you've only one storage place—your body —and, if you've hoarded too much, the storage place is unsightly.

But that is an esthetic view. There are

physical reasons of greater urgency. For each surplus pound of flesh you need a mile of new capillaries and blood vessels. Consider how much extra mechanical work the heart must perform in order to supply the blood for vast areas of useless fat! Moreover, the heart's efficiency is impaired by deposits of fat surrounding it. No wonder that obese people so often have heart and circulatory disturbances!

Surplus fat deposits also interfere with the regulation of body-heat. Thus, fat people are prone to skin infections. They are particularly liable to chafing, because, being restricted in their activities and forced to sit in one place, their skin becomes hot, red, and tender. They perspire freely, and their skin, steeped in the sweat retained, often cracks and bleeds. Overlapping areas of skin, irritated by sweat, rub together.

The result, as anybody who has suffered from it will testify, is extremely unpleasant. The unpleasantness is greatest where the fat causes the greatest pressure and friction: under the breasts, between the thighs and buttocks, beneath the overlapping folds of skin, under the arms.

There's another facet to the matter. A famous dermatologist (specialist in diagnosing and treating skin disorders) once called the skin "the mirror of the body." Its color and texture sensitively record the condition of the body. Because they overindulge in rich and difficult-to-digest foods, fat people continually "break out"—that is, they're chronically subject to skin eruptions ranging from the disagreeable to the dangerous.

Remember, too, that your body, the fat-warehouse, can't be conveniently left be-

hind—you must carry it with you where-
ever you go. It's a burden. It not only
makes you tired sooner, but also causes
you trouble with regard to feet, legs, and
spine. Posture suffers almost inevitably as
a result.

Insurance companies consider overweight "a very serious disability" (to quote
the Metropolitan Life Insurance Company). The death rate, all insurance companies sorrowfully report, increases as
overweight increases. Not only do fat people tend to get certain diseases like diabetes, gout, kidney and heart trouble, but
also they have greater difficulty in recov-
ering from all diseases.

The psychological effect of overweight,
too, should be taken into account. Obese
people are not usually happy people, in
spite of the popular opinion to the con-

[31]

trary. They are debarred from any number of normal pleasures, and they feel frustrated by the fact. In addition, they suffer pangs of guilt, because, whatever their pretenses, they know that they wallow in "seas of tumultuous flesh" at their own option. *They can be thin.*

CHAPTER VI

In Which, by Considering the Calories, You See the Limitations of Exercise as a Way of Whittling Weight

———— ◆◗●◗◆ ————

WE'VE MENTIONED calories once or twice. Definition is necessary, since many people have a muddled notion of what they are. A calorie is simply a measure of energy— just as a pound is a measure of weight or a foot is a measure of distance.

More technically, a calorie is the amount of heat required to raise a pound of water four degrees Fahrenheit. "What," you ask, "has raising pounds of water to do with losing pounds of fat?" Everything.

It's calories that make you fat. An ounce of cane or beet sugar contains more calories than a couple of large heads of lettuce, and therefore the sugar is more fattening than the heads of lettuce. It isn't bulk that counts: it's the calories. You can eat an insignificant amount of foods high in calorie content and grow fat; or you can eat a considerable amount of foods low in calorie content and grow thin. Plainly, then, any sensible reducing diet requires that you cut down on the calories by cutting down on foods which are packed with calories.

Since people get fat because their energy intake is greater than their energy output, mightn't a good way to reduce be to increase energy output? That is, mightn't it be as well "to eat as before, but to exercise more?" Theoretically, yes; and in fact some exercise is advisable while re-

[*34*]

ducing because it tends to increase the rate of metabolism—the rate at which the body uses up energy.

But even if obese people could exercise without putting an undue strain on their hearts (and arches), exercise would not be a very effective method of weight reduction.

CONSIDER: A two hundred pound man uses up only one calorie in climbing a fifteen-foot ladder! If you played a tough set of tennis, you'd use up 150 calories; have an ice-cream soda after the set, and you'll have gained your lost weight back with interest! Have a slice of bread and butter (about an ounce of bread and a quarter of an ounce of butter) and you've derived enough energy to climb 1,980 feet—or more than one and one-half times the height of the Empire State Building!

CHAPTER VII

In Which You Come to Realize the Futility—or the Danger—of Mechanical Reducing-Methods

————◆◄●►◆————

FIRST, A WARNING: *under no circumstances* ought you take gland-extracts or drugs, or anything resembling either, without the advice and supervision of a physician. They're potent—and potentially dangerous in direct proportion. Not until you've attempted a rational diet should you even consider them. If you're under the illusion that simply by taking thyroxin or another extract you can grow slim, you need disillusioning: a low calorie diet is nevertheless a required part of the reducing method.

Reducing salts, teas, and patent medicines of all sorts are scarcely less bad. Most of them substitute a program of diarrhea for a program of diet. They're either useless or harmful—and nothing in-between.

Bath powders and bath salts, soaps, salves, and pastes—all the manifold external applications—are a waste of effort and of money. They're so plainly innocuous that it's hard to see why people fall for them.

Hot baths, vapor baths, Turkish, Finnish, and Russian baths—all are similarly unavailing. The body loses water in such baths, and of course there's an apparent loss of weight as a consequence. But within twenty-four hours (less, if you drink more than you normally do because of the bath) you'll get all the water and all the weight back. If you're weighing in for a fight and trying to make the poundage, by all means try one form of sweat-bath or another. Otherwise—don't.

Cold baths are somewhat helpful, since they stimulate metabolism. But few people can stand them; and if you've a heart condition, stay away.

Mechanical appliances, such as trusses, belts, corsets, and mechanical massagers, vibrators, and rolling-pins effectively help you get rid of money but not of fat. Massage is excellent—for the masseur; it will do you a piddling amount of good.

No—there's no comfortable way to whittle your weight: you'd better stop looking for an escape and start looking at our diet program.

[38]

CHAPTER VIII

In Which You Are Reminded of the Basic Food-Facts

———— ◄◆►◄ ————

THE BODY needs energy and warmth. It needs to build and repair tissue. It needs to protect itself against disease. Different kinds of food supply these needs.

Fats and carbohydrates supply the first need—energy and warmth. Both are rich in calories—fats are opulent with them, having about two and a quarter times the calorie value of carbohydrates. People who are extremely active *physically* (football players but not chess players), or people who live in cold climates, need lots of fats and carbohydrates. The lists below include the important sources of each.

Foods Rich in Fat

bacon	doughnuts	nuts
butter	fats of meats	oil
chocolates	fried foods	pies & pastries
cream	ham	pork
cream soups	lard	sausages

Foods Rich in Carbohydrates
(Starches and Sugars)

beer, ale, stout (and all alcoholic drinks)	ice cream
	potatoes
	rice
bread	spaghetti
canned fruits	sweet carbonated drinks
chocolates	
dried beans & peas	sweets
dried fruits	thickened soups & sauces
flour	

Proteins supply the second need—repair and building.

Below is an abridged list of foods containing proteins:

Foods Rich in Protein

beans	fish	lentils
bread	fowl	milk
cheese	gelatin	nuts
egg white	lean meat	peas

Minerals and vitamins supply the third need—protection against disease. Minerals help regulate the body machinery and keep it running smoothly and efficiently. They also, like the proteins, aid in the building and repair of body tissue. The following list tells in what foods you can find each of the important minerals.

Foods Rich in Minerals

A. *Calcium:*
   beans, broccoli, cauliflower, cheese, cream, egg yolk, kale, milk, nuts, sardines, turnip greens.

B. *Copper:*
   bran, liver, lobsters, mushrooms, nuts, oysters, shrimps.

C. *Iodine:*
   cod-liver oil, iodized salt, sea food.

[*41*]

D. *Iron:*

> asparagus, beans (dried), beet greens, bran, chard, dandelions, egg yolk, peas, lettuce, liver, nuts, oatmeal, oysters, parsley, soybeans, turnip greens, watercress, whole wheat.

E. *Manganese:*

> bananas, beans, beets, bran, celery, cucumbers, dates, liver, oatmeal, onions, peas.

F. *Phosphorus:*

> beans, bran, cheese, eggs, fish, grains, liver, meat, milk, oatmeal, shellfish, peas, yeast.

G. *Potassium:*

> bran, cheese, corn, eggs, fish, legumes, liver, macaroni, meat, milk, nuts, oatmeal, prunes, raisins, seafood, whole grains, yeast.

H. *Sodium:*

> bread, cheese, clams, crackers, oysters, wheat germ, whole grains.

The vitamins are mysterious food elements necessary for health. We know that they're necessary for health, because if they're not in the food you eat, diseases like scurvy, rickets, beri-beri, pellagra and impairments of function like sterility and night-blindness occur. They're mysterious because nobody knows just how they work "their wonders to perform." What is important is that you get each of the vitamins, and enough of each. Since people in general don't know where the different vitamins are to be found, we've made this list longer and more extensive than the others.

Vitamins in Foods
Vitamin A
BEST SOURCES

(* following an entry indicates an especially valuable source.)

Apricots, beans (green) , beet tops, butter,* fish-liver oils (cod, halibut, shark) ,* fish roe, leafy green vegetables (beets, broccoli, collards, dandelion greens, kale, spinach, turnip greens, watercress,* liver,* mangoes, milk, papayas, peaches (yellow), peas (green), peppers (green), potatoes (sweet) , prunes, pumpkin, squash.

GOOD SOURCES

Asparagus (green), bananas, cantaloupe, corn (yellow), currants (black), onions (green), oranges, pecans, tomatoes.

Vitamin B₁ (*Thiamine*)

BEST SOURCES

Bread (whole wheat),* cereals (whole grain), corn, egg yolk, legumes (dried), nuts, organ meats (heart, kidney, liver), pork,* rice (brown), wheat bran, wheat germ,* yeast (brewers', dried).

GOOD SOURCES

Asparagus, avocado, beans (green), cabbage, carrots, cauliflower, fish roe, grapefruit, leafy green vegetables, leeks, mangoes, mushrooms, okra, oranges, oysters, papayas, parsnips, pineapple, plums, potatoes (white and sweet), tangerines, tomatoes.

Vitamin B₂ (G, *Riboflavin*)

BEST SOURCES

Almonds, bran, buttermilk, cheese (cheddar), eggs, leafy green vegetables, meats (lean and

organ: heart, kidney, liver) ,* milk, oysters, peanuts, pecans, prunes, salmon, wheat germ, whey,
yeast (dried) .*

FAIR SOURCES

Apricots, avocados, bananas, beans, cheese
(cream) , corn, lentils, oatmeal, papayas, potatoes (sweet) , peas, whole wheat.

Niacin (*PP factor*)
(*Nicotinic Acid*)

BEST SOURCES

Beef (fresh, corned) , buttermilk, collard, kale,
meats (lean and organ: heart, kidney, liver),*
peanuts, peas, pork, poultry, rabbit, rice polish-
ings, salmon (canned) , tomato juice (canned) ,
tongue, turnip greens, veal, yeast.*

GOOD SOURCES

Cabbage (green) , beans (kidney) , cod, cowpeas, egg yolk, haddock, herring, milk, mustard
greens, peas (dried) , soybeans, spinach.

Pantothenic Acid
BEST SOURCES

Beef, broccoli, buttermilk, egg yolk,* kale,
liver,* milk, molasses, potatoes (sweet) , squash
(zucchini) , whey, yeast.

[*45*]

GOOD SOURCES

Bran (wheat & rice), cowpeas, milk, potatoes, peas, pumpkin (canned), salmon (canned), soybeans, tomatoes.

Vitamin C (*Ascorbic Acid, Cevitamic Acid*)
BEST SOURCES

Broccoli, Brussels sprouts, cabbage (green, raw), cantaloupe, cauliflower, citrus fruits (grapefruits, lemons, limes, oranges),* currants (black), grains (sprouted), greens (dandelion, mustard, turnip), kale, kohlrabi, paprika, parsley, peppers, pimentos, spinach, strawberries,* watercress.

GOOD SOURCES

Asparagus, chard, currants (red), Lima beans, papayas, peas (fresh), pineapples, tomatoes.

Vitamin D

Fish-liver oils (cod, halibut, shark), irradiated foods.

Vitamin E

Egg yolk, fruit,* lettuce,* milk, wheat germ.*

Vitamin K

Cabbage, carrot tops, cauliflower, egg yolk, kale, liver, soybean oils, spinach, tomatoes.

[46]

CHAPTER IX

In Which You Learn About Protective Foods

———◆◀●▶◆———

Do YOU EAT foods high in fuel value but low in building and protective value—are your foods calorie-rich, but protein-, mineral, and vitamin-poor? If so, you'll have to take in lots of calories in order to take in the proper amount of the other necessary elements. "As long as such foods play a prominent part in our diets," one authority says, "we must choose between generous curves and jumpy nerves."

But, of course, such foods need not play a prominent part in your diet. You can cut

[47]

down on calories without cutting down on proteins, minerals, and vitamins. (Remember: cut calories mean cut weight.)

Here's the way you must alter your present eating habits in order to lose weight.

1. You must reduce your fat intake greatly.

During the course of your diet, you'll be practicing what dietitians call "cannibalistic consumption" of fat. You can conveniently draw from the fat deposits you've made till now.

2. You must reduce your carbohydrate intake considerably.

You aren't able to eliminate carbohydrates, though, because you'll be burning stored fuel—body-fat. And if body-fat is burned when carbohydrates are lacking, acidosis develops. (Acidosis is a condition resulting from the accumulation of too

[48]

much acid.) One excellent slogan to re-member is: "no calories without vita-mins." Don't, for example, eat any over-refined foods (such as white flour, white sugar, white cereals), since the vitamins and minerals have been refined right out of them. Again, don't eat foods that have been over-soaked or over-cooked, since vitamins B, B₂, C, and niacin have been soaked or cooked away.

3. You must not decrease your protein intake.

The building and repair functions of protein foods are as important now that you're reducing as they were before—more important, if anything. Besides, pure pro-tein is probably not at all fattening, since it more than pulls its own weight: it stimu-lates metabolism and promotes the oxida-tion of body-fat.

[49]

4. You must increase your mineral and vitamin intake.

Protective foods are plainly of large importance while you're changing your regimen. Follow these recommendations.

a.) *Drink three or four cups of milk a day.* If you don't like your milk straight, take it in soups, cereals, or other cooked dishes.

b.) *Have one serving a day of yellow vegetables and of leafy green vegetables.* These contain Vitamin A, which is not destroyed to any extent by cooking.

c.) *Have at least two servings a day of other vegetables and fruits*—one of a citrus fruit (orange, grapefruit, lemon) or tomato, and one of another fruit or vegetable.

d.) *Eat at least four eggs a week* (cooked soft, preferably). Eggs are valuable for iron and high quality protein, as well as for certain vitamins.

e.) *Help yourself to one or two servings of whole grain cereal products.*

f.) *Eat meat—or some other high protein food—once a day.* Meat is the best form of protein since it's animal protein, like yours, and therefore the most readily converted.

[50]

CHAPTER X

In Which You Get a Brief Introduction to the Ways of Weight

——————◆◀◉▶◆——————

"HOW MUCH OUGHT I to weigh?" There's no question more frequently asked of the reducing specialist. But there's no categorical answer which can be given. What you should weigh depends, among other things, on how old you are, on how you're built (whether you've a small, medium, or large frame), and on how well mineralized your skeleton is.

However, the U.S. Navy has adopted a convenient height-weight rule. Men five feet tall should weigh 110 pounds; for every additional inch in height, simply add five and one-half pounds. Thus, according to the rule, a man five feet-two inches tall should weigh 121 pounds; a man five feet-six inches tall should weigh 143 pounds; a man six feet tall should weigh 176 pounds.

For women, the height-weight rule is a little different. Women should weigh 100 pounds if they're five feet tall; for every inch that they're taller, add five pounds. Thus, a woman five feet-two inches should weigh 110 pounds; a woman five feet-six inches should weigh 130 pounds; a woman six feet tall should weigh 160 pounds.

Men or women of heavy build, may require a ten percent leeway. Thus, a man five feet-six inches tall who is of heavy build may weigh 157 or 158 pounds; a woman of the same height and heavily built may weigh 143 pounds.

The same allowance—ten percent of bodyweight—is required for people having a light build. Thus, a man with a light build who is five feet-six inches tall may weigh only 128 or 129 pounds; a woman of the same height who has a light build may weigh only 117 pounds.

Remember that a ten percent variation, even a fifteen percent variation, from the normal is not to be considered serious. And remember, too, that all pounds-to-inches ratios are only approximate.

Nevertheless, the Navy's guiding rule is a good one, and other estimates aren't significantly different. Below we reproduce the Metropolitan Life Insurance Company's weight tables. These list the desirable weights for men and women 25 years old or older. The tables are based on hundreds of thousands of cases. (Note that the

[53]

weights are given for both men and women "as ordinarily dressed.")

WOMEN

Weight in Pounds According to Frame
(as ordinarily dressed)

Height (with shoes on) Feet Inches		Small Frame	Medium Frame	Large Frame
4	11	104–111	110–118	117–127
5	0	105–113	112–120	119–129
5	1	107–115	114–122	121–131
5	2	110–118	117–125	124–135
5	3	113–121	120–128	127–138
5	4	116–125	124–132	131–142
5	5	119–128	127–135	133–145
5	6	123–132	130–140	138–150
5	7	126–136	134–144	142–154
5	8	129–139	137–147	145–158
5	9	133–143	141–151	149–162
5	10	136–147	145–155	152–166
5	11	139–150	148–158	155–169

MEN

Weight in Pounds According to Frame
(as ordinarily dressed)

Height (with shoes on) Feet Inches		Small Frame	Medium Frame	Large Frame
5	2	116–125	124–133	131–142
5	3	119–128	127–136	133–144
5	4	122–132	130–140	137–149
5	5	126–136	134–144	141–153
5	6	129–139	137–147	145–157
5	7	133–143	141–151	149–162
5	8	136–147	145–156	153–166
5	9	140–151	149–160	157–170
5	10	144–155	153–164	161–175
5	11	148–159	157–168	165–180
6	0	152–164	161–173	169–185
6	1	157–169	166–178	174–190
6	2	163–175	171–184	179–196
6	3	168–180	176–189	184–202

CHAPTER XI

In Which You Are Given a Series of Do's and Don't's

––––––◄◄●►►––––––

IN THE BACK of this book there's an extensive list of foods in 100 calorie portions. From it, you can choose what substitutes you like. One hundred calories of any food are no more and no less fattening than a hundred calories of any other food.

But you'll have to choose foods with bulk to them, foods that will stay with you, foods that are chock-full of the desirable elements. That's the explanation of the list of do's and don't's which follows.

A. Help yourself!

Fresh Fruits

blackberries	oranges
cantaloupe	papayas
cranberries	peaches
gooseberries	pineapples
grapefruit	strawberries
honeydew melon	watermelon
lemons	

Fruits Canned Without Sugar

apples	loganberries
apricots	peaches
blackberries	pears
cherries	pineapples
grapefruit	raspberries
grapes (white)	strawberries

Vegetables

asparagus	cucumbers
beet greens	eggplant
broccoli	endive
Brussels sprouts	green pepper
cabbage	lettuce
cauliflower	mushrooms
celery	mustard greens

okra	summer squash
radishes	Swiss chard
sauerkraut	tomatoes
sea kale	watercress
string beans	

B. Help yourself—lightly!

(These fruits and vegetables contain more sugar than those listed in A.)

Fresh Fruits

apples	guava
apricots	huckleberries
blueberries	nectarines
cherries	pears
currants	raspberries

Vegetables

beets	pumpkin
carrots	rutabagas
kohlrabi	squash
leeks	turnips
onions	

C. Once a day!

(An average portion of any of these.)

bananas	cereal
beans	corn

grapes	peas
macaroni	plums
noodles	potatoes
parsnips	rice

D. In moderation!

meat (a small serving twice a day)

egg (one egg for breakfast, two eggs as a meat substitute)

fish (a small serving as a meat substitute)

milk (3 cups or 1½ glasses a day of skim milk —that is, milk with the cream drawn off)

E. Sparingly!

bread (two average-size slices a day)

cream (one tablespoonful a day)

butter (one and one-half squares a day)

F. Avoid!

pork, bacon, fatty meats, pies, pastries, candy, sugar, syrup, honey, jams, preserved fruits (saccharine may be used as a sweetening agent)

salad oil and cooking fat (mineral oil may be substituted for both)

wine, whisky, beer, ale, stout

CHAPTER XII

In Which You Look at Menu-Outlines

————◄◄●►►————

MENUS FOR YOUR 1,000-calorie diet are
given in the next chapter. However, you
may prefer to plan your own meals. Here,
then, is an outline. On pages 108–117
you'll find a table of foods in 100-calorie
portions. Employ it to make what substitu-
tions you choose—but be careful to keep
the calorie-count.

Incidentally, don't be overly generous
in calculating portions. Remember that a
small serving means one and one-half to

two ounces, an average serving means three ounces, and a large serving four to five ounces. You'll become adept at calculating by eye in a short time, but in the beginning you'll probably have to weigh portions.

SPECIMEN MENU

Breakfast

Orange

Egg, 1

Toast (1/2 slice)   Butter (1/2 square)

Coffee with one tablespoon of cream

Skim Milk (or Buttermilk), 1/2 glass

Lunch

Meat or fish, small serving

or Eggs, 2

Vegetables (from the "Help Yourself" list)

1 or 2 servings

Bread (1/2 slice)   Butter (1/2 square)

Fruit (from the "Help Yourself" list)

Tea or coffee (without cream or sugar)

Skim Milk (or Buttermilk), 1/2 glass

[61]

Dinner

Broth or clear soup
Meat or fish, average serving
Potato (one small)
Vegetables, 2 or 3 servings
Bread (one slice)   Butter (1/2 square)
Fruit
Tea or coffee (without cream or sugar)
Skim Milk (or Buttermilk), 1/2 glass

The menu probably includes more than you normally eat in the course of a day. Yet the calorie total is certainly far less.

And the menu may be varied to suit your eating habits. Are you an inveterate before-bedtime snacker? Then leave a reserve of a hundred or so calories for snacking. First, though, see whether black coffee or tea (with saccharine, if you like your drinks sweet) doesn't satisfy you almost as well. Coffee and tea (and saccharine) contain no calories, and you may imbibe them freely. Bouillon, too, may be used liberally.

Some ingenuity won't do any harm. Your meat, fish, or fowl can be prepared differently for each meal. Boiling, broiling, baking, and roasting are equally allowed. Even frying is not forbidden—if mineral oil (a non-fattening substance) is used for the frying. (Mineral oil, by the way, can be used as a base for salad dressing too.) Condiments—such as salt, pepper, spices, vinegar—may be used in reasonable quantities. So your meals need be neither less filling nor less tasty than before.

CHAPTER XIII

In Which You Reconsider the Calories: Two Sets of Tested Menus

———————◆◂◉▸◆———————

A MODERATELY active man expends about 3,000 calories a day and a moderately active woman about 2,400. Of course, these are average estimates. A seamstress might use up only 1,800 calories, whereas a washwoman might use up almost twice that number. A desk-worker might burn 2,500 calories doing his job, and a day-laborer 3,500-4,000 calories doing his. An extremely active housewife might, in the course of her day, work off almost as many calories as a carpenter or painter.

We're going to recommend a 1,000-calorie diet. How much weight you'll lose by following it obviously depends on how much greater than a thousand your calorie expenditure is. *If you are normally active, however, we can promise that you'll lose a minimum of two pounds a week.* (A little later we'll tell you of the *tested and proved* results of this diet.)

You may want to know why 1,000 calories was decided upon rather than some other figure. The reason is simple. A very low calorie diet—say 600 calories—would mean so small a bulk that you would be hungry all the time. Moreover, you would be too weak and energyless to work effectively.

On the other hand, a much larger calorie diet—say 1,800 calories—would mean a trifling loss of weight. You would quickly

[65]

become discouraged and abandon the diet.

The 1,000-calorie diet that we prescribe has enough bulk to stay acute hunger-pangs. It has enough energy value to prevent you from feeling faint or exhausted. And it keeps your morale up because it gets results.

The diet was tried on a group of students at the University of Illinois—with marvelous success. None of the people who tried the diet suffered unduly from hunger or fatigue—or from any other cause—and the diet left no bad effects of any kind.

The average amount of weight lost was two pounds a week, though one dieter lost almost twice as much and another only a little better than half. One girl weighed 217 pounds at the beginning of the diet; twenty-four weeks later she had sloughed

[66]

off sixty-four and an eighth pounds. But she thought 154 pounds still overweight and set her goal at 145. She reached it easily and comfortably.

The point to emphasize is that *the diet is effective in practically every case,* whether a little or a lot of weight has to be lost.

THE UNIVERSITY OF ILLINOIS MENUS

(1,000 calories per day)

SUNDAY

First Day

Breakfast

Grapes, about 25

Coddled egg, 1   Broiled Bacon, 2 slices

Whole Milk, 1 glass   Coffee (black)

Dinner

Roast chicken, 3 thin slices (3 oz.)

Cranberry sauce, 1 tablespoon

Cauliflower, 1/4 small head

String beans, 1/2 cup

Hearts of lettuce, 1 large serving with 3/4 tablespoon French dressing

Supper

Cold Sliced Chicken, 2 small slices

Celery and carrot sandwich, 1 small

Sliced orange, 1   Whole milk, 1 glass

[*68*]

MONDAY

Second Day

Breakfast

Grapefruit, 1/2 medium
Baked egg with grated cheese, 1 egg
Whole milk, 1 glass   Coffee (black)

Luncheon

Broiled meat patties, 2 1/2 oz.
Brussels sprouts, 1 cup
Tomato salad, 1 small tomato on 3 leaves of
     lettuce with lemon juice or vinegar
Whole milk, 1 glass

Dinner

Broiled sirloin steak, 1 medium serving (3 oz.
     of lean meat)
Mashed potatoes, 1/4 cup, made with 1/2 table-
     spoon butter
Celery curls, 2   Lettuce salad, with dress-
     ing
Canned peaches, 2 small halves

TUESDAY

Third Day

Breakfast

Sliced orange, 1   Poached egg, 1
Buttered whole wheat toast, 1/2 thin slice with
    1/2 teaspoon butter
Whole milk, 1 glass   Coffee (black)

Luncheon

Cheese souffle, 1 serving (about 3 1/2 oz. or 2
    large serving spoonfuls)
Peas 1/2 cup
Cabbage slaw, 3/4 cup with sour cream dressing
Canned pears, 2 halves

Dinner

Pot roast of beef, 2 slices (3 oz.)
Stewed celery, 2/3 cup
Asparagus salad, 1 serving (6 to 8 cups on let-
    tuce) with dressing
Baked custard, 1/2 cup

WEDNESDAY

Fourth Day

Breakfast

Cantaloupe, 1/2 small
Boiled egg, 1
Buttered whole wheat toast, 1/2 thin slice with
    1/2 teaspoon butter
Whole milk, 1 glass   Coffee (black)

Luncheon

Green pepper stuffed with meat, 1
Creamed cucumber, 1/2 cup
Bread, 1/2 thin slice with 1/2 teaspoon butter
Fruit cup, 2/3 cup (grapefruit, apple, & peaches)
Whole milk, 1 glass

Dinner

Broiled liver, 2 slices (3 oz.)
Stewed Lima beans, 1/4 cup
Sliced tomatoes, 1 medium
Carrot & pineapple salad in gelatin, 1/2 cup
    with dressing
Vanilla ice cream, 1/4 cup
Coffee (black)

[*71*]

THURSDAY

Fifth Day

Breakfast

Sliced orange, 1 medium
Coddled egg, 1
Whole milk, 1 glass   Coffee (black)

Luncheon

Jellied shrimp & tomato salad, 1 serving with
     mineral oil dressing
Cabbage au gratin, 2/3 cup
Whole milk, 1 glass

Dinner

Broiled beef tenderloin, 1 medium serving (3
     oz.)
Riced potatoes, 1/2 cup
Pickled beet salad, 5 small beets on 3 leaves of
     lettuce
Baked apple, 1 medium
Coffee (black)

FRIDAY

Sixth Day

Breakfast

Fresh peach, 1 large   Baked egg, 1
Buttered whole wheat toast, 1 thin slice with
    1/4 teaspoon butter
Whole milk, 1 glass   Coffee (black)

Luncheon

Consomme, 2/3 cup
Dry toast, 1/2 thin slice
Puffy omelet, 1 small (1 egg)
Apple, raisin, cabbage salad, 3/4 cup with sour
    cream dressing

Dinner

Broiled haddock, 1 medium serving (3 oz.)
Buttered peas and carrots, 1 cup with 1/4 table-
    spoon butter
Pear and cottage cheese salad, 1/2 pear and 1
    tablespoon cheese, with dressing
Saltine, 1   Whole milk, 1 glass

SATURDAY

Seventh Day

Breakfast

Fresh plums, 3 medium
Poached egg, 1
Whole milk, 1 glass   Coffee (black)

Luncheon

Rutabagas au gratin, 1 cup
[Any other of the vegetables listed on pages 57–
   58 will do as alternative.]
Hot pickled beets, 5 small
Hearts of lettuce salad, 1 large
Cottage cheese balls, 2 tablespoons
Whole milk, 1 glass

Dinner

Broiled pork tenderloin, 1 medium serving
   (3 oz.)
Parsley potatoes, 1/2 medium with 1 teaspoon
   butter
Tomato aspic salad, 1 serving (1/2 cup tomatoes) with dressing
Fresh grapes, about 25

[*74*]

The University of Illinois 1,000-calorie menus that you've just scanned had highly gratifying results. The United States Navy, too, employed 1,000-calorie diets for its overweight personnel—and with success as marked.

You can use the Navy diet which we give on the seven pages following instead of the Illinois menus, if you prefer. Or perhaps some particular Illinois menu doesn't appeal to you; you may substitute any one of the Navy menus. Or you can use the Illinois and Navy menus in sequence or alternately (and thus have a fourteen-day diet) if you don't like to plan your own meals. (For easier distinction, the Navy Menus are printed in small letters throughout, whereas the University of Illinois Menus have the first letter of each entry capitalized.) •

THE NAVY MENUS

(1,000 calories per day)

FIRST DAY

Sunday

Breakfast

1/2 grapefruit	1/2 pat butter
soft cooked egg	coffee
1 slice whole wheat	1 oz. cream
toast	

Dinner

tomato juice   beets
broiled chicken   orange sherbet
summer squash
1/2 slice whole wheat bread   1/2 pat butter
tea or coffee

Supper

1 lamb chop   carrot & cottage cheese
green beans   salad
spinach
1/2 slice whole wheat bread   1/2 pat butter
1 glass skim milk

SECOND DAY

Monday

Breakfast

orange slices
poached egg
1/2 slice whole wheat toast   1/2 pat butter
coffee   1 oz. cream

Luncheon

bouillon
roast tenderloin
peas   cole slaw
1/2 slice whole wheat bread   1/2 pat butter
1 glass skim milk
sugar-free peaches

Dinner

tomato juice
lean broiled ham
asparagus
beets
sugar-free pineapple salad
orange and grapefruit cup
1/2 pat butter
1 glass skim milk

[77]

THIRD DAY

Tuesday

Breakfast

orange juice   scrambled egg
1/2 slice whole wheat toast   1/2 pat butter
1 oz. cream   coffee

Luncheon

tomato bouillon
roast veal
baked squash
wax beans
head lettuce with lemon
sugar-free applesauce
1/2 slice whole wheat bread   1/2 pat butter
1 glass skim milk

Dinner

cottage cheese and deviled egg
wax beans
peas
sliced tomato salad
sugar-free apricots
1/2 slice whole wheat bread   1/2 pat butter
1 glass skim milk

[78]

FOURTH DAY

Wednesday

Breakfast

1/2 grapefruit
3 strips crisp bacon
1/2 slice whole wheat toast   1/2 pat butter
1 oz. cream   coffee

Luncheon

bouillon
roast lamb
spinach
stewed tomatoes
sugar-free peach and cream cheese salad
1/2 slice whole wheat bread   1/2 pat butter
1 glass skim milk

Dinner

skim celery soup
small steak
carrots   green beans
cabbage and green pepper salad
sugar-free pineapple
1/2 slice whole wheat bread   1/2 pat butter
tea

[79]

FIFTH DAY

Thursday

Breakfast

orange halves
soft-cooked egg
1/2 slice whole wheat toast   1/2 pat butter
1 oz. cream   coffee

Luncheon

consomme
veal cutlet
asparagus   boiled cabbage
grapefruit and pimento salad
sugar-free peaches
1/2 slice whole wheat bread   1/2 pat butter
1 glass skim milk

Dinner

lean Canadian bacon
green beans   stewed tomatoes
celery hearts
sugar-free baked apple
1/2 slice whole wheat bread   1/2 pat butter
1 glass skim milk

SIXTH DAY

Friday

Breakfast

1/2 grapefruit
poached egg
1 slice whole wheat toast   ½ pat butter
1 oz. cream   coffee

Luncheon

skim milk
broiled lake trout
baked squash
spinach with lemon   orange salad
sugar-free cherries
1/2 slice whole wheat bread   1/2 pat butter
tea

Dinner

tomato juice
cold salmon
green beans   beets
sliced tomatoes & lettuce
sugar-free fruit cup
1/2 slice whole wheat bread   1/2 pat butter
1 glass skim milk

[*81*]

SEVENTH DAY

Saturday

Breakfast

orange juice
scrambled egg
1 slice whole wheat toast ½ pat butter
1 oz. cream coffee

Luncheon

broth
roast beef boiled cabbage
carrots head lettuce with lemon
sugar-free pineapple
1/2 slice whole wheat bread 1/2 pat butter
1 glass skim milk

Dinner

broiled lamb chop with tomato
spinach
cauliflower salad
orange and grapefruit cup
1/2 slice whole wheat bread 1/2 pat butter
1 glass skim milk

CHAPTER XIV

In Which You Are Warned of the Pitfalls on the Way to Slenderness

———◄◄●►►———

DURING THE COURSE of your diet, you may backslide occasionally. Then do penance. If you've accepted a dish of ice cream at a bridge party and thus eaten 250 calories more than you should have, cut 125 calories from your menu for the next two days. Remember that 250 excess calories means an extra ounce of fat for you. And the ounces add up—22.81 pounds in a year, to be exact.

Close your calorie account each week.

If on Monday you've had four hundred unallowable calories' worth of peanuts, see that the ledger is balanced by Sunday. But —best—see that you don't ever get on the debit side of the ledger: keep to 1,000 calories a day.

Don't be discouraged if you lose less than the two pounds promised during the first week. When the body begins to use its own fat, the body's water balance is changed. Consequently, you may gain in water what you lose in fat. But that condition is only a temporary one.

Sometimes you'll feel hungry, especially in the early stages of the diet. Your digestive apparatus hasn't become accustomed to your new manner of eating. It's not hunger, as one authority remarks: it's a feeling misinterpreted for hunger—"merely a gastric memory of more carefree days when the only index of satiety was distension of the stomach." As your digestive system comes to accept your diet, the feeling will gradually disappear. In the meantime—have a cup of coffee (minus cream or sugar) and a cigarette.

If your weight loss is less than two pounds a week (after·the first week or so), examine your conscience. Have you been cheating—taking a casual candy here, a friendly beer there? If you haven't, see a doctor. If, on the other hand, your weight loss is greater than three pounds a week, increase your calories by a hundred or two.

Don't be misled by food-faddists. When they hear you're on a diet, they beat a path to your door even if you live in the wilderness and don't build a better mousetrap. They'll tell you that you ought to subsist only on vegetables if you really want to lose

[*85*]

weight, or that you ought to concentrate on bran, buttermilk, beans, bananas— Bunk! Heed them not. The diet you're on has been tried by the U.S. Navy, by schools, colleges, hospitals; and always successfully.

Enlist the aid of your family and friends. Ask them not to tease or to tempt you. If they're gorging themselves on pie-à-la-mode and making ecstatic gestures the while, they'll reduce your resolve to reduce. Have them understand the importance of your being earnest in the effort you're making.

CHAPTER XV

In Which You Get Some Post-Diet Hints

——— ◄◄◆►► ———

AFTER YOU'RE through dieting, what then?

Well, you can abandon your Spartan re-gime, certainly. You can't, probably, go back to the indiscriminate guzzling of chocolate nut-fudge sundaes. Of course, you can have the gooey stuff on occasion, but it can't be a regular stop in your food-schedule.

However, you probably won't want it to be, now that you've undermined the psy-chological causes for abnormal eating and learned a lot about what constitutes an intelligent diet. You'll find normal calorie-consumption (about fifteen to twenty calories per day for each pound of body weight) quite all you feel the need for.

Besides, you'll have an ally continually encouraging you to keep permanent the break with your old eating habits. And the ally? Your mirror, which will reflect a gracefully trim individual. You.

Some Psychological Profiles

———◆◀●▶◆———

HERE ARE a half-dozen case histories—reconstructions of the past lives of people in order to find out why they're behaving as they are. Our case histories are psychological profiles, so to speak, not full portraits. They're abbreviated, condensed, so that the salient features become apparent.

Probably none of the people sketched will have precisely your problem; but almost certainly one or more of them will have a problem that will be a glass through which you can see yours more clearly. The cases are all suggestive: read them carefully to extract the clues that will help you solve your own problem. If you really want it solved, if you're really willing to work towards solving it, it can be—it will be!

Jean J.

Jean J. is nineteen, and pretty in spite of her poundage. An only child, she's been babied all her life by both her mother and father.

Her parents have a lot to do with her excessive weight—though they and she would deny it in all sincerity. Don't they frequently ask her to stop stowing away candy, cake, and carbonated drinks? They do; but that's not the point. . . .

Let's take a quick look at the parents. The father is a mild, suppressed individual. He's the fellow who brings home the bread and the bacon, but the mother is plainly the head of the household. She's a vigorous, aggressive woman, capable of making decisions—and she makes them!

That her decisions appear to be well-founded and intelligent is not relevant. This is relevant: her mother is stifling Jean's desire to mature. Jean is adjusted to a state of extreme dependence. She doesn't want to grow up. She doesn't want to take on all the burdens that maturity—and marriage—would mean.

However, she's pretty and fellows are asking her for dates. Her parents urge her to accept some of the invitations—all her friends go dating. She, herself, thinks that she *ought* to—but she doesn't *want* to.

Here, then, is the situation: Along with her reluctance to go out with men—because that might result in marriage, in her being weaned from her mother, in being forced to shoulder the burdens of adult life—along with this reluctance, Jean feels that it's right and proper to go out with men, and everybody agrees that it is.

Jean has a real conflict. It's not her fault; nevertheless, she's the only one who can resolve it. Unfortunately, she's never developed the force that is required. Instead of meeting her problem, she tries to evade it. She begins to eat far more than she needs to balance her energy-expenditures —far more than she ever has eaten before.

Why?

For two reasons. First, she is eating to allay her anxiety, the anxiety caused by thoughts of being forced to leave her mother and comfortable dependence. The second reason is a little harder to appreciate: Jean is eating excessively to render herself ineligible for dates and men, to become grossly fat so that she won't be asked for dates.

[92]

Does that mean Jean does this con-
sciously, fully realizing what she's doing?
Does she say: "I'll eat like a pig and consequently I'll look like one; and then,
because I'll be so unattractive, men will
never ask me out on dates"?

Of course not!

It's an *unconscious attempt to fulfill her
wish to remain dependent* on her mother
that's operating. Jean would be aghast if
the matter were put in plain terms.

Rose R.

If you were asked to describe Rose,
you'd say that she was thirtyish, obviously
fat, and, not less obviously, quite nervous.

The reason for Rose's obesity, as she'll
tell you in all frankness should you ask, is
that she enjoys eating, and that the eating
tends to "quiet her nerves."

But Rose won't easily be able to answer if you ask her why she's nervous.

On the surface, there seems to be little enough cause. Her parents, with whom she lives, are comfortably fixed and her life involves only a minimum of friction.

But let's dig a bit beyond the surface and see what we can turn up.

As a child, Rose was rather sickly and her parents (her mother especially) were continually on the watch to see that she did not exert herself too much. It is very easy for a necessary carefulness of this kind to slide into a nagging overcarefulness. Rose was kept firmly in leash, restrained from engaging in even the mild play which would have harmed her not at all.

A pattern of caution was traced; and even after Rose had outgrown her childhood malady, the pattern was not erased.

"Vigilance" was the watchword her parents stuck to and were stuck with. Almost invariably, such an attitude is not fixed to the specific causes which generated it. Such attitudes overflow, they extend to other relationships—and particularly to sex.

Thus, when Rose reached puberty (the beginning of adolescence) her parents seized the opportunity to scare her concerning the physiological changes taking place. They figured that if Rose were worried enough, she'd refrain from doing things they firmly believed were bad for her.

The parents succeeded in making Rose worry enough. With the best intentions in the world (the kind hell is supposed to be paved with) they turned Rose into a nervous young woman: emotionally unstable, afraid, neurotically disturbed.

Worry makes Rose eat as much as she does. Food does yield, along with energy, a certain feeling of well-being, a temporary surcease from worry. Worry—a baseless worry—makes Rose nervous and fat at the same time. Nor is hers an exceptional case. As one writer says: "For every individual who worries himself thin there are three who worry themselves fat."

Lawrence L.

Lawrence feels badly about being obese. Then why doesn't he cut down on the fifteen hundred surplus calories he takes in each day? Why doesn't he eliminate at least the pies and potatoes he stows away? Why does he sneak snacks?

The answer to all these questions is: Lawrence doesn't like being fat, but he hates to attempt even the minimum effort involved in getting thin.

[96]

Lawrence, as a matter of fact, is allergic to anything resembling activity— His vocation and his hobby is idleness.

"A lazy lummox" you say? Maybe . . .

Lawrence's mother and father were immigrants. To make their way, they worked long and hard in an alien country and at unpleasant tasks. The little luxuries didn't come until they were past enjoying them.

Lawrence was their only child, and in him they attempted to realize their dreams of a life they'd never lived—a life of ease and of idleness. In a very real sense, he was their substitute-life.

In the old country black bread was the food of the poor, white bread of the well-to-do. Lawrence always ate white bread. Sweets and pastries were the luxuries of the wealthy. They were staple foods for Lawrence. The rich were idle. His parents encouraged Lawrence in his indolence. Fatness symbolized carefree wealth, and Lawrence fulfilled his parents' desires in that respect, too.

Lawrence is going counter to society's established and recognized standards. They're standards which he accepts in theory, though not in the practice impressed on him by his parents. Of course, therefore, he's unhappy, bored, ashamed.

Emily M.

She's in her early twenties and she's come to the big city from Prairietown (population 350). She's lost, bewildered by the apparently confused activity.

The movies help her to escape. Quietly curled on her seat in the comfortably dark theatre, Emily identifies herself with the heroine who is lovely, sought after, happy, and eventually triumphant.

Seated in the theatre, Emily chews caramel after caramel. The movies and the munching are of a piece. When Emily was a child, she'd often go to the movies armed with munching-material.

What Emily's trying to do now is go backward in time, back to the days of her childhood. Then she was happy with her family and friends, adjusted to the simple pattern of small-town life.

If Emily restricted her caramel consumption to the motion picture theatre, her weight-problem would be minor. After all, a movie does not last indefinitely. Emily, however, must make her exit from the warm dark theatre to the bright and bustling world of reality. And the things which caused her to try for the escape-via-movies are still at work.

She goes to her room, reads, listens to

the radio, or perhaps just day-dreams till
bedtime. Always, these activities are ac-
companied by the incessant, almost auto-
matic consumption of the caramels and
other candies for which she has developed
a "passion." They have become the chief
source of satisfaction and comfort for
Emily, the only source that she can readily
tap. They've displaced life.

Arthur A.

Admittedly, Arthur A. hasn't an easy
lot: his wife is a shrill shrew, his job's dull
and pays poorly. Discontent, bored, gen-
erally maladjusted, Arthur does what so
often we have noticed others doing: he eats
to adjust the balance between what he
hasn't and what he wants—and he takes
to drinking heavily, whereas before he'd
been only a casual or "social" drinker.

[*100*]

So far, Arthur's case parallels the others we've studied: the same mechanism is at work, a futile effort to compensate for the things desired and not possessed. However, here's the strategic difference: Arthur will tell you—lucidly and logically —just why he overeats. He knows the jargon. "Insecurity," "overprotection," "overcompensation"—all the special terms of psychodietetics fall glibly, trippingly from his tongue.

Listen to his little monologue: "I drink more firewater and eat more food than I should, considering what my energy expenditure—and income—is. Sure. But I'm doing both because I'm discontent. There's nothing 'queer' or 'psychoneurotic' about my behavior. Only, when the reasons are imaginary do you have to call in the psychiatrist. The psychiatrist! He's a humorous individual, all right—a very funny man. He never changes his tune. Is there any argument between you and your environment? Without hesitation, the psychiatrist will tell you you're wrong. How about the environment? Isn't that ever at fault? Look: change my circumstances and watch how quickly I stop eating—and drinking—to excess."

Arthur rests his case. Instead of using the insight he has acquired as a fulcrum for overthrowing an unhappy condition, he uses it as a base for self-justification, an excuse for continuing to eat and drink intemperately.

Leona O.

Leona's started her fifth decade, and things she's not willing to accept are happening. The word "climacteric" or

[*102*]

"menopause" sums them up. The physical changes that occur are well known: there's little point in rehearsing here the "hot flushes," sweating, headaches, and sensations of dizziness going with the altered glandular state which marks the end of a woman's biologic service to her species.

There are usually psychological symptoms accompanying the menopause: anxiety, sleeplessness, depressive reactions, periods of irritability and excitability. And in Leona's case these are intensified because she refuses to accept the inevitable. All her vanity—which is considerable—protests against relinquishing her reproductive function.

She's been spoiled—as a child by her fond parents, as a woman by her submissive husband. She's always been charmingly and gracefully feminine, and all the

[*103*]

homage rendered to her beauty she's considered as her due. Now, nature's reminding her that she's growing older and less attractive sexually.

She revolts; unwilling to renounce her femininity, to accede to the irresistible, she attempts to preserve the illusion of youthfulness. Her visits to the beautician's, the hair-dresser's, the milliner's, and the dressmaker's become frantically frequent. She behaves like a coy young thing—especially when young men are around.

However, though Leona is flighty, she's by no means dim-witted. She realizes, after a while, the futility of fighting what must be. She gives in to the climacteric process wholly, becomes apathetic, depressed. No longer restrained by thoughts of ruining her figure, she indulges lavishly in fattening foods. In violent reaction to her previous behavior, she seems to be trying to render herself as unalluring as possible.

Of course, her depressed moods increase in frequency and intensity. Leona begins to imagine that her friends are gloating over her biologic misfortune, that her husband is seeking his pleasure elsewhere.

In order to get Leona right, you must not imagine that it is her inability to bear children in itself that's bothering her so deeply. It's that her inability to bear children has become a symbol of what she considers her secession from femininity.

*   *   *

What advice may be given to these six people?—In every case, the start of the answer is: know yourself!

But what about Arthur? He knew himself, and yet the knowledge did him no good.

Knowledge, then, is only part of the answer. *Act on the knowledge*—that's the rest of the answer. Use knowledge not as a basis for rationalization, for creating better excuses, but for the purpose of helping yourself. Arthur must remember that man makes his own environment, too. Arthur's an unfortunate person; granted. Yet by intelligent action he can make things significantly better for himself. By persisting in his present course, he'll make them significantly worse.

Consider Leona, for example: Millions of women of her age have noted, unhappily, that the life processes were beginning to wane, that youth was gone and age coming. But they've turned to other creative pursuits. Some have developed a real interest in art, music, or literature. Others have returned to school to resume work for a degree long forgone. Still others have taken a larger part in organizational work of various kinds. In general, they've revived interests that were overshadowed by the reproductive function. They've sought for—and found—substitute satisfactions; they've attained to a new contentment.

Obesity is more than the condition of being overweight. It's also a warning that something is wrong with your emotional life. The purpose of this book is to tell you not only how to lose weight (though we hope it does that too) but also how to take advantage of that warning.

FOOD VALUES IN 100 CALORIE PORTIONS

Fruits

Apple	1
Apple sauce	⅓ cup
Apple, baked	½ large, 2 tbsp. juice
Apricots, sweetened dried or stewed	¼ cup
Banana	1 medium
Blackberries	1 cup, 50 berries
Cantaloupe	1 melon, 5 in. diameter
Cherries	1 cup
Dates	4
Figs	2 medium
Grapes	20
Grapefruit	½
Orange	1 large
Peach	2 large
Pear	2 large
Pineapple canned	2 slices, 2 tbsp. juice
fresh	2 slices, ¾ in. thick
Plums	4 medium
Prunes (stewed)	3 medium, 3 tsp. juice
Rhubarb (stewed)	½ cup
Strawberries	1⅔ cups
Tangerines	2
Watermelon	¾ inch slice, 6 in. diameter

Fruit Juices

Grapefruit	1 cup
Lemon	1 cup
Orange	¾ cup
Grape	⅔ cup
Pineapple (canned)	½ cup

Cereals

Shredded Wheat	1 biscuit
Puffed Rice	1⅔ cups
Corn Meal	⅔ cup
Cream of Wheat	⅔ cup
Farina	¾ cup
Oatmeal	¾ cup
Rice	¾ cup
Wheatena	¾ cup

Breads

White	2 slices
Whole wheat	½ inch thick of small
Gluten	sandwich loaf
Rye	3 in. by 3½ in. square
Corn	2 in. by 2 in. by 1 in.
Biscuit (baking powder)	2 small
Rolls	1
Griddle Cakes	1, 4 in. diameter
Waffles	½, 6 in. diameter
Muffins	¾, 2¾ in. diameter
Toast	1⅓ slice, thin
Zwieback	5 pieces: 3¼ by 1¼

Crackers

Educator	12
Graham	2½
Oatmeal	7
Oyster	24
Saltines	6
Soda	4

Soups

Asparagas (cream)	½ cup
Bean	½ cup
Bouillon	4 cups
Celery (cream)	½ cup
Chicken	1 cup
Clam chowder	¾ cup
Consomme	4 cups
Corn (cream)	½ cup
Oyster Stew	½ cup
Pea	⅗ cup
Tomato	1 cup
Vegetable	1 cup

Vegetables

Asparagus	20 stalks
Beans (lima)	½ cup
(string)	2 cups
Beets	1 cup cooked
Broccoli	2⅓ cups
Cabbage	2 cups

Cauliflower	1 small head 4½ in. diameter
Celery	30 stalks
Cole slaw	1 cup
Corn, canned	⅓ cup
on cob	2 ears 6 in. long
Cucumbers	2: 7 in. long
Lentils	⅓ cup
Lettuce	2 heads
Onions (raw)	3 to 4
(creamed)	2
	100 calorie portions
Peas, green, shelled	¾ cup
Potatoes, sweet	½ medium
sweet, glazed	½ small
white baked	1 medium
mashed	½ cup
Radishes	30 medium
Rice, steamed	¾ cup
Rutabagas	1 large
Spinach, cooked	2½ cups
Squash, Hubbard	1 cup
Summer	½ squash, 5 in. diameter
Succotash, canned	⅓ cup
Tomatoes, canned	2 cups
fresh	2-3 medium
Turnip greens	1⅔ cups
Turnips	2 cups

Fish and Shellfish

	100 calorie portions
Clams	10 medium
Codfish, creamed	½ cup
Crab meat	¾ cup
Lobster meat	¾ cup
Mackerel, Spanish, broiled	Cross-section 2½ in. on back
Oyster stew	⅓ cup
Oysters	10 medium
Salmon, canned	½ cup
Sardines, canned	4 large
Scallops, fried	2 large
Shrimp	20 shrimp (¾ cup)
Smelts	2 large
Tuna fish, canned	⅓ cup

Meats and Poultry

	100 calorie portions
Beef, corned, boiled	slice 4 in. by 2 in. by ½ in.
dried	4 thin slices
hamburger	2½ oz.
liver, broiled	2 oz. (medium slice)
rib, lean, roasted	2 oz. (medium slice)
round, lean, potted	2⅓ oz. (medium slice)
sirloin steak, broiled	2 oz. (medium slice)
stew, with vegetables	½ cup
Bologna sausage	slice 2⅛ in. diameter, ½ in. thick

Chicken, broiler	½
roast	slice 4 in. by 2½ in. by ¼ in.
Ham, boiled	slice 5 in. by 5 in. by ⅛ in.
Hash	¼ cup
Lamb chops, broiled, lean	one chop 2 in. by 1¼ in. by ¾ in.
leg, roast	slice 3⅓ in. by 4¼ in. by ⅛ in.
Liver, broiled	2 oz. (medium slice)
Mutton, leg, roast	slice 3 in. by 3¾ in. by ⅛ in.
Pork chops, broiled, lean	½ chop
sausage	1⅔ sausages (small)
Tongue	2 small slices
Turkey	small portion
Veal leg, roast cutlet	⅖ of a normal serving slice 3 in. by 2 in. by ¾ in.

Salads

Crab meat	⅓ serving
Egg	⅖ "
Potato	½ "
Tomato and Cucumber	⅝ "
Tomato and Lettuce	½ "
Sardine	⅓ "
Waldorf	⅖ "

Date and Nut with May- onnaise	¼ serving
Chicken	¼ cup·

Dairy Products and Fats

Whole Milk	⅝ cup
Skimmed "	1⅛ cups
Buttermilk	1⅛ cups
Cream 18% fat	¼ cup
40% fat	1⅔ tbsp.
Cheeses, cottage	5½ tbsp.
full cream	2 in. by 1 in. by ⅜ in.
Neufchâtel	2 tbsp.
Roquefort	1½ by 1¼ by ⅛ in.
Swiss	4½ by 3½ by ⅛ in.
Oleomargarine	1 tbsp.
Olive oil	1 tbsp.
Butter	1 tbsp.

Eggs

Boiled or poached	1 large
Fried	1 small
Scrambled	¼ cup
Omelette	1 egg

Beverages

Cocoa	½ cup
Coffee	1 cup, 2 tsp. sug. and 1 tsp. cream

Postum	1 cup, 2 tsp. sug. and 1 tsp. cream
Tea	1 cup, 2 tsp. sug. and 1 tsp. cream
Ginger ale, 6 oz. bottle	1½ bottles

Desserts

Angel Cake	slice 2 in. by 2 in. by 2 in.
Apple snow	1 cup
Apple tapioca	¼ cup
Apple dumpling	⅓ med.
Bread pudding	¼ cup
Brown Betty	⅕ cup
Cake, layer	2½ by 2½ by 1 in.
plain	1¾ in. cube
Charlotte Russe	½ cup
Chocolate Blanc Mange	¼ cup
Coffee Jelly	1 cup
Cornstarch Pudding	¼ cup
Cream Puff	¾ cream puff
Custard cup	⅓ cup
" soft	⅓ cup
Fig Pudding	⅓ cup
Floating Island	⅛ cup
Fruit Cake	1 in. cube
Gingerbread	1 in. by 2 in. by 2 in.
Jello	½ cup
Junket	⅓ cup

Macaroons	2 macaroons
Ice cream	¼ cup
Plum Pudding	1 in. cube
Pies, apple	sector 1½ in. at circum.
custard	" 2 in. " "
lemon	" 1 in. " "
mince	" 1 in. " "
pumpkin	" 2 in. " "
squash	" 2 in. " "
Prune souffle	⅖ cup
Rice Pudding	¼ cup
Tapioca	⅓ average portion
Sherbet	¼ cup
Strawberry Shortcake	⅓ average portion

Nuts

Almonds	12 to 15
Brazil	2
Butter	4 to 5
Hickory	15
Peanuts	20 to 24
Pecans	12 meats
Walnuts	8 to 16 nuts
Chestnuts	7, average size
Coconut (desiccated)	¼ cup

Miscellaneous

Baked beans	⅓ cup
Candy	
chocolate creams	1 piece

fudge	1 in. cube
milk choc.	2 in. by 1 in. by ½ in.
Cheese souffle	½ cup
Cranberry sauce	¼ cup
Cream sauce	⅙ cup
Dressing (stuffing)	⅙ cup
Gravy	2 tbsp.
Hash	2 oz.
Hard sauce	1 tbsp.
Honey	1 tbsp.
Ice cream soda	⅓ av. soda
Jam	1 tbsp.
Jelly	1 tbsp.
Macaroni, cooked	1 cup
" and cheese	1 tbsp.
Maple syrup	1 tbsp.
Mayonnaise	1 tbsp.
Molasses	1½ tbsp.
Olives	4 large
Peanut butter	1 tbsp.
Pickles	1 tbsp.
Popovers	1
Raisins	¼ cup
Rarebit	1½ tbsp.
Stuffed pepper	1 pepper
Sugar	3 tsp.
Sundaes	⅓ av. portion
White sauce	¼ cup

Printed in the United States
134660LV00003B/13/A